ISBN 1 85103 323 8

Originally published as *Antonio Vivaldi Découverte des Musiciens* jointly by Editions Gallimard Jeunesse & Erato Disques.
© & ℗ 1999 Editions Gallimard Jeunesse & Erato Disques.
This edition first published in the United Kingdom jointly by Moonlight Publishing Ltd, The King's Manor, East Hendred, Oxon OX12 8JY
& The Associated Board of the Royal Schools of Music (Publishing) Limited, 24 Portland Place, London W1B 1LU.
English text © & ℗ 2002 by Moonlight Publishing Ltd & The Associated Board of the Royal Schools of Music.
Printed in Italy

Antonio

VIVALDI

FIRST DISCOVERY - MUSIC

Written by Olivier Baumont
Illustrated by Charlotte Voake
Narrated by Michael Cantwell

Can you imagine a city with water and canals instead of streets? The city of Venice, in Italy, is like this. In Venice, people travel in boats called gondolas. It is one of the most beautiful places in the world. The Venetians love fun, music,

SINFONIA FOR STRINGS AND CONTINUO, RV 146, 3RD MOVEMENT, PRESTO
THE FOUR SEASONS, SPRING, 1ST MOVEMENT, ALLEGRO

dancing, parties and dressing up – particularly at Carnival time. On 4th March 1678, shortly after the Carnival, Venice was shaken by an earthquake. The same day, one of the greatest Italian musicians was born: Antonio Vivaldi.

MAKE AN INSTRUMENT

Have you ever tried making a musical instrument? With a reed you can make a little flute. What kind of instrument do you think you could make with some bits of wood and some gut or wire strings pulled very tight?

Antonio grows up near the church of San Martino, in a poor part of the city where the streets are busy and noisy with so many activities.

ARSENAL

He plays in one of the little squares in the neighbourhood which smells of baking and clean washing. Close by is the arsenal, where huge cannons are made. It is fascinating to watch them being built!

SINGING WHILE YOU WORK

Did you know that in the old days different shopkeepers and tradesmen each had their own tunes. This meant you could tell who was who in the streets. Can you invent a tune for what you would like to be?

Antonio's father has more than one job. He is a barber and also a baker. But best of all, he enjoys making music. He becomes a violinist in the orchestra of St Mark's when Antonio is seven years old. The little boy often goes

FRIENDS AND MUSIC

Have you ever played music with your friends? It can be tricky but it's great fun. Some instruments go very well together, like the violin and the harpsichord, or the flute and the guitar...

3 CONCERTO, RV 558,
1ST MOVEMENT, ALLEGRO MOLTO

to listen to his father playing with the other musicians. They all recognize Antonio because he has bright red hair, just like his father. Later he will be nicknamed 'il rosso', 'redhead'.

From that time on, Antonio can think of nothing else but learning about music. His father teaches him how to play the violin, which he loves from the start. Sometimes he goes to St Mark's to listen to the great composer

4 GLORIA, RV 588, 'GLORY TO GOD'

Giovanni Legrenzi. He falls in love with the sound of singing voices and the organ making music together. At thirteen, he begins to write his own sacred music.

IMITATE THE VIOLIN

There are four strings on a violin. When you pluck them or stroke them with a bow, they will sound four notes rising up from G to D to A to E. You can easily find the same notes on a keyboard instrument and hum them.

Antonio is the eldest child in his family. His younger brothers are often fighting, bickering and getting into trouble. Antonio worries about them a lot. While he is busy with his music, they are quarrelling and

5 CONCERTO FOR TRUMPET, STRINGS AND CONTINUO,
IST MOVEMENT, ALLEGRO

fighting in the street. Later, one of the brothers is arrested after using a knife in a fight with a baker's son. He is sent away from home for five years.

15

MUSIC OR NOISE?

Try to think of all the noises you could hear in a quarrel: very loud voices, shouting, a door slamming, feet stamping on the ground, things being thrown...

Antonio's family do not have much money. Antonio decides to become a priest. That way he will have a job and security. He begins his religious training very early. At fifteen and a half he has to have his hair cut and

COMPOSING AND COPYING

Vivaldi could write music very quickly. He copied it out himself, because having music printed was very expensive. Have you ever tried copying out a piece of music into a notebook marked up with staves? A stave is the pattern of lines and spaces on which music is written.

6 CONCERTO FOR ORGAN, BWV 596, BY J. S. BACH,
ADAPTED FROM VIVALDI'S 'HARMONIOUS INSPIRATION', FINALE

his head shaved in a way that is special to priests.
Fortunately, in his new life Antonio still has plenty of
time to write music and to play his beloved violin.

Antonio is now very well-known in Venice: he often performs to great applause from the public. At twenty-five he becomes a music teacher at the Ospedale della Pietà, a school for girls. There is an orchestra and a choir, which he leads from the harpsichord or on the violin. Through his music Antonio has the art of making those around him happy.

GOING TO A CONCERT

Have you ever been to a concert? When the whole orchestra is playing, the conductor stands right in front, centre stage. His back is turned to the audience because he has to use both hands to direct the musicians, who play facing the audience. Why don't you pretend to conduct the next piece?

7 CONCERTO FOR TWO MANDOLINS, STRINGS AND CONTINUO, RV 532, 3RD MOVEMENT, ALLEGRO

Today

as in the past

Vivaldi's

music

is played

and loved.

THE FOUR SEASONS

Vivaldi composed over 400 concertos for various instruments. *The Four Seasons* for violin and orchestra is a set of four concertos which depict spring, summer, autumn and winter. A concerto is a piece of music in which one or more leading instruments play in conversation with the orchestra. It is Vivaldi who popularized the concerto in three movements: quick, slow, quick. Listen how, in the first movement of *Autumn*, Vivaldi manages to portray villagers dancing and singing in their harvest festival. In the second concerto, for oboe and orchestra, the oboist seems to be imitating the human voice.

20

Vivaldi was himself a virtuoso violinist. That's why the violin is often the lead instrument in his concertos.

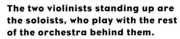

The two violinists standing up are the soloists, who play with the rest of the orchestra behind them.

---

8 THE FOUR SEASONS, AUTUMN, IST MOVEMENT, ALLEGRO
CONCERTO FOR OBOE, STRINGS AND CONTINUO, RV 465, OP. 7 NO. I, 2ND MOVEMENT, LARGO

CELLO SONATA

Chamber music is music which is meant to be played in the home. It only needs a small group of musicians to play it. It has always been very popular because it allows friends to make music together. Vivaldi wrote a lot of chamber music: sonatas for violin, cello and flute, or for the different sizes of recorder, often with a harpsichord accompaniment. In the piece of music you are about to hear, notice how the instruments converse with one another, just like actors do on stage in a play.

In times when recordings did not exist, playing music with friends was an enjoyable way of getting to know pieces. The harpsichord (below) is a keyboard instrument on which the strings are plucked. It was very popular in Vivaldi's time.

9 SONATA NO. 5 FOR CELLO AND HARPSICHORD, RV 40, 2ND MOVEMENT, ALLEGRO

STABAT MATER

Venice has always been full of churches. Sacred music is still performed in many of them. You can hear the organ being played and choirs singing all over Venice. All his life Vivaldi wrote sacred music: motets and music for different parts of the mass such as the *Kyrie*, the *Gloria* or the *Credo*, or hymns such as the *Stabat Mater*, which describes the pain experienced by the Mother of Christ at the death of her son. For the *Stabat Mater*, Vivaldi composed very expressive music filled with great pain and sadness.

Venetians were very religious people, and their various festivals almost always began or ended in a church.

Vivaldi composed many sacred works for the Ospedale della Pietà; the students went to church services every day.

24

ORLANDO FURIOSO

Imagine a stage with props, scenery and dancers; add to this singers in magnificent costumes who tell a story, and a whole orchestra, all directed by a conductor. That is what makes up an opera. Vivaldi composed over forty operas, which had huge audiences. For these performances Vivaldi was not only the composer, but also the conductor and the producer. What's more, he selected the musicians, the singers and the dancers and chose the designer. Composer and impresario, all in one! In the aria you are about to hear, the hero, Orlando, sung by a woman, expresses his pride as a warrior and his desire to find Angelica, with whom he has fallen in love.

26

Already in the seventeenth century a huge amount of space was needed backstage in opera houses for storing scenery.

The story of *Orlando furioso*, written by Ariosto at the beginning of the sixteenth century, was the inspiration for several composers: Lully and Handel as well as Vivaldi.

MOONLIGHT PUBLISHING

Translator:
Penelope Stanley-Baker

ABRSM (PUBLISHING) LTD

Project manager:
Leslie East

Language consultant:
Cathy Ferreira

Text editor:
Lilija Zobens

Editorial supervision:
Caroline Perkins & Rosie Welch

Production:
Simon Mathews & Michelle Lau

English narration recording:
Ken Blair of BMP Recordings

ERATO DISQUES

Artistic and Production Director:
Ysabelle Van Wersch-Cot

KEY: **t** = top   **m** = middle   **b** = bottom
       r = right   **l** = left

PHOTOGRAPHIC ACKNOWLEDGEMENTS

Archiv für Kunst und Geschichte, Paris/Cameraphoto **16**. Verona Amphitheatre (Photo Bisazza) **26b**. Ph. Coqueux/Specto **20m**, **20b**, **24b**. G. Dagli Orti **8**, **10**, **15**, **18**, **19**, **20t**. Giraudon **22tr**, **23**. Photograph by Erich Lessing **13**. Collection Musée de la Musique/Cliché Albert Giordan **22tl**, **22b**. A. Pacciani/Enguerand **24m**, **26m**. Photo RMN **25**. Photo RMN/Gérard Blot **21**. Photo RMN/Béatrice Hatala **7**, **24t**. Photo RMN/R.G. Ojeda **27**. Frédéric Sapey-Triomphe **26t**.

CD

1. Carnival on water
Sinfonia for strings and continuo in G major, RV 146, 3rd movement, Presto
I Solisti Veneti
Directed by Claudio Scimone
4509 96382 2
℗ Erato Classics SNC 1978

The Four Seasons, Spring, RV 269, Op. 8 No. 1, 1st movement, Allegro
Andrew Manze, violin
The Amsterdam Baroque Orchestra
Directed by Ton Koopman
4509 94811 2
℗ Erato Disques SAS 1996

2. Playing outdoors
Serenata, Eurilla's aria: 'La dolce auretta'
Daniela Mazzucato, soprano
I Solisti Veneti
Conducted by Claudio Scimone
4509 97417 2
℗ Erato Classics SNC 1984

3. Redheads, like father like son
Concerto in C major, RV 558, 1st movement, Allegro molto
I Solisti Veneti
Conducted by Claudio Scimone
2292 45203 2
℗ Erato Classics SNC 1984

4. Starting music
Gloria in D major, RV 588, 'Gloria'
English Bach Festival Chorus
Choirmaster, Nicholas Cleobury
English Bach Festival Baroque Orchestra
Conducted by Michel Corboz
℗ Erato Classics SNC 1975

5. Bickering brothers
Concerto adapted from Sonata Op. 2 No. 4 in A flat major for trumpet, strings and continuo, 1st movement, Allegro
Maurice André, trumpet
Orchestre de Chambre Jean-François Paillard
Conducted by Jean-François Paillard
4509 92124 2
℗ Erato Classics SNC 1965

6. In holy orders
J. S. Bach
Concerto for organ in D minor, BWV 596, adapted from Vivaldi's L'estro armonico, Finale
Marie-Claire Alain, organ
0630 15343 2
℗ Erato Classics SNC 1980

7. Virtuoso musician and teacher
Concerto for two mandolins, strings and continuo in G major, RV 532, 3rd movement, Allegro
Ugo Orlandi, Dorina Frati, mandolins
I Solisti Veneti
Conducted by Claudio Scimone
4509 92239 2
℗ Erato Classics SNC 1984

8. The concerto
The Four Seasons, Autumn, RV 293, Op. 8 No. 3, 1st movement, Allegro
Andrew Manze, violin
The Amsterdam Baroque Orchestra
Conducted by Ton Koopman
4509 94811 2
℗ Erato Disques SAS 1996

Concerto for oboe, strings and continuo in D minor, RV 465, Op. 7 No. 1, 2nd movement, Largo
Marcel Ponseele, oboe
The Amsterdam Baroque Orchestra
Conducted by Ton Koopman
4509 94811 2
℗ Erato Disques SAS 1996

9. Chamber music
Sonata No. 5 in E minor for cello and harpsichord, RV 40, 2nd movement, Allegro
Paul Tortelier, cello
Robert Veyron-Lacroix, harpsichord
2292 45658 2
℗ Erato Classics SNC 1965

10. Sacred music
Stabat Mater, RV 621, 'Stabat Mater'
Naoko Ihara, alto
Lisbon Gulbenkian Orchestra
Conducted by Michel Corboz
4509 91936 2
℗ Erato Classics SNC 1977

11. Opera
Orlando furioso, Act 1, Orlando's aria: 'Nel Profondo'
Marilyn Horne, mezzo-soprano
I Solisti Veneti
Conducted by Claudio Scimone
2292 45147 2
℗ Erato Classics SNC 1978

JOHANN SEBASTIAN BACH
LUDWIG VAN BEETHOVEN
HECTOR BERLIOZ
FRYDERYK CHOPIN
CLAUDE DEBUSSY
GEORGE FRIDERIC HANDEL
WOLFGANG AMADEUS MOZART
HENRY PURCELL
FRANZ SCHUBERT
ANTONIO VIVALDI